SUSAN

1

In the parlour:
my grandmother and her sister,
heads bent
over a homemade Ouija board,
fingers touching lightly
as the small water glass
spells out their future

They ask about marriage, children, love;
death is a word they don't consider

2

Five years pass:
Susanna, now 22,
laid out in the same parlour

My grandmother
cannot approach the coffin

For weeks
she cannot even enter the room;
dreams of a board,
a shard of glass
deep in the letter D

ENDANGERED SPECIES

At a footwear trade show
my grandmother admires
an untamed pair of shoes:
black and high-ankled,
sewn of the softest antelope

The man in charge
notices her interest, offers her
the shoes for sex

She says nothing,
stares down the double-barrel eyes

Within the hour
(although the cost
will leave its imprint
on next month's meals)
she has bought the shoes
elsewhere

Prances her way
blithely past the barter man
who aims his eyes at her,
pulls the trigger

IRONIC

Arms crossed, the sister-in-law
sits by the window, watches
a man enter the house next door

It is my grandmother's house;
the man is not my grandfather

No light but the green numbers
on the radio, silence
except for the soft murmur of war news,
everything suspect

What the in-law doesn't see:
my grandmother's hand
resting on a small boy's head
as he sleeps in her lap;
the man, eyes closed
at the far end of the room,
listening

The next day the in-law
calls my grandmother a whore,
says she needs a bull,
not a husband

A comment for which
my grandfather slaps her
hard on the mouth, a man
defending one woman
against another

20

WHY I AWOKE AT 3:30 A.M.

Because need was approaching
and I was restless

Because something in me
refused to be rested

Because the house was silent
but my dreams were talking

21

SHUTDOWN

Caught
in the headlights of crisis
you stand
paralyzed, unable
to move, not
to move

The decision itself
has immobilized you,
and so you stare
at the light, keep staring
as it fast approaches, threatens
to engulf you

Remember: the vehicle
that owns this light
will soon run you over

And the only person
who can startle you
is you

DOING FIRE

This is a conscious act,
an act of awareness

It requires focus and centering,
courage and fear; courage
mostly

Doing fire is not easy
nor for the faint of heart

It's more than making

When you've done fire,
you know what it is to be
destroyed, purified,
rekindled

Simultaneously

23

GAUNTLET

I throw down my heart
like a gauntlet

It lies at your feet,
a precocious invitation

Will you pick it up?

And if you accept the challenge,
which challenge will it be,
to heal it or to shatter it?

This is the chance I take
when I engage you

Above us, fate
circles like a hawk

Safety, risk

Out of this dichotomy
something slouches toward
understanding, waiting
to be born

WHAT I KNOW ABOUT YOU

That you appease the demons,
every one

That you are not serious
about love

That you are gentle
in your non-seriousness

That when passion slips into you,
far and *late* and *seldom*
are no longer words that govern you

That when the rhythm of destiny
pulses in your deepest self,
you finally relinquish control
and love me

25

THE WHOLE STORY

You tell me you will meet your ex
for dinner, you do not want
to hold secrets, you will let her know
you love me, you will give her
the whole story, as it is

The dinner happens, and something else:
the plot takes a new direction

You walk out of it, start
a new fiction, become unavailable
for conversation, find excuses
for why you can't see me

Suddenly, I'm on the wrong side
of safety, arguing
with a text I continue to read
but am no longer writing with you

You have become the sole author

So now it's my turn:
let's have dinner

Tell me the whole story,
as it was

Is

MY HEART HEARS YOU DREAMING

Years pass but I do find you;
your open self is still my fate,
such joy your mouth is speaking

I sight-read each day as it comes,
listen carefully to learn by beat
the song of your softest breathing

And within the silence that is love,
my heart hears you dreaming

27

I am friend not foe, a soul
who treads gently through
the griefs you've been keeping

A lover who loves your fluent hands,
evening sky in summer:
your blue eyes simply being

And though I am not with you now,
my heart hears you weeping

Through the landscape of my fear,
I braille my way toward trust,
weary but believing

Yet despite the journey I have made,
the music weakens,
the distance is not receding

And within the silence that is love,
my heart hears you leaving

28

DAFFODILS

You bring me daffodils,
seven rows of seven
packed tightly
into a promising square of spring

I place them on the kitchen wine rack
where they bloom
suddenly, tiny yellow flames
at first
like candle tips, then
insurgent bursts of yellow
multiplying eventually
into a miniature field of suns,
an eye playground

But as the weeks pass
the fires die down;
there is nothing now
but a profusion of slumping stems
hanging heavily downward

You have not seen
any of this, nor do you see
the care with which
I follow instructions, cut back
the wilted stalks, store
the bulbs in paper

Will you be here in the fall
when I plant them,
these reminders of potential?

I gaze at the daffodils,
think of us

30

I have always been a sucker
for symbolism

SEPARATE VENUES

You and I are always
at a different place
at the same time

Tonight, for instance,
you listen to your friend
sing jazz at a Toronto bar
while I, in my study,
listen to Bocelli
sing Italian romance

You light a cigarette,
order another drink,
converse with strangers
(an art you have perfected)

I tuck my son into bed,
pour another glass of wine,
read *Artist on Fire*

Fire has been my home motif lately—
a place rather than an element

This has been my journey: to rise
out of deep water into air, grow wings,
fly over flames

I have yet to be grounded

And your journey,
what has it been?

Earth, water, air, fire:
which is your element?

32

Not air
since you and I
are always at a different place
at the same time

WHAT IT'S ABOUT

It's about the slow dismantling
of hope, the casting aside
of desire

It's about the cost
of that desire

It's about presence
and absence, having
and not having,
meticulous chaos

It's about time and timing,
and death, the ultimate
timelessness

33

It's about standing
at the corner of Myth and Truth,
a dangerous intersection, no light
to count on

It's about the quicksand
pull of memory, you
on the right side of the bed, your profile
silhouetted in 3 a.m. darkness

It's about the heart,
brought to its knees—
every time

TIMING IS EVERYTHING

The sun knows this, and the moon

My heart also, as it clocks its way
forward

And because timing is everything,
I wonder what's too soon, too late,
what chance missed altogether

What if I had called you
at a different hour or on a different day,
in a different year perhaps?

Would you have loved me less or more,
or not at all?

Would I be sitting at this midnight desk,
mourning your arrivals, how they're played now
in a lower key, your leaving already audible
even as you enter?

Would I notice the wane of enthusiasm,
the barometric drop in passion?

If I had cherished your eyes
in a different season,
would my heart be different, or your hands?

My savage heart, your knowing hands

THE END OF THE ENDINGS

We agree: sex
complicates things, and ruined love
strips away more than armour

The crack of mistrust widens, chasms
finally into an exit from desire

You have been my seasons in hell,
one after the other

So how will it break, finally,
this uncanny connection
between us?

The heart storms its answer

What it comes down to in the end:
we don't choose whom we love;
we don't choose whom we don't love
either

BY UNION STATION
I SAT DOWN AND WEPT

I didn't really, but I felt like it,
there
at the corner of Bay and Front, waiting
for the light (and you)
to change

The light changed, you didn't
and so
I crossed the street,
wondered about words:
green   forward   go

Knew that in my crossing
I was walking both from and toward
the two-faced Janus
that is love

36

A COMMON STORY

There will come a point
when you can go no farther,
not in these shoes,
not on this road

You know this, yet continue

The weather has changed,
and so has the landscape

What was once warm and avuncular
has now shifted toward cold;
the threat of rain is present always

On both sides the forest grows denser;
it's hard to discern the individual trees

You're afraid to be alone at nightfall,
walk faster though your feet hurt

You long to turn back, but it's too late;
the road rolls up behind you like a carpet

How you got here is a common story:
someone promised you safety,
and you believed him

THE PATH OF TENDER HEROES

The path of tender heroes
is not lonely, nor is it
fraught with sadness

It is not angry
nor is it ashamed
for there is no rage or embarrassment
in loving the journey

Wherever your foot falls,
the ground sings;
whenever the wind rises,
your heart swells

38

These are the rhythms
of you in the world,
the world in you

Be grateful for the fierce darkness,
the unnerving light, for both
will teach you

The path of tender heroes
is strewn with compassion
and lined with the stuff of stars

Along the way, one sign only:
the walking is in the walking

A FRIEND SENDS AN E-MAIL
IN MARCH

I've had it with winter,
with pretending that I love
my husband, with wondering
if the man I do love
loves me at all, never mind
how much

I've had it with waiting
for messages, for Godots
who don't arrive, for signs
from the universe

I've had enough of silence,
existential angst and bullshit

I no longer feel like being stoic

To put it simply:
I'm fed up

39

TIRED

You're tired of your life turning
into something you don't recognize

Tired of men pathologizing love,
arranging it in their own best interest;
tired
of sitting sell-bound in restaurants
feigning wonder at exploits
neither compelling nor infamous

You're tired of the sell,
always the same:
the lure of lust,
a promise of future

And when it's over
it's never really over; they return
seeking solace in your comfort zone,
your patient allegiance

Keep you guessing
what it is they want from you,
what it is you can give them

You're tired
of this unfinished business with men,
have begun to dream
of taking yourself somewhere,
arriving

NIGHT SHIFT
AT THE WOMEN'S SHELTER

I picture you in a pool of light,
oasis in the darkness; around you
rooms of sleeping women, you alone awake,
guardian of dreams, keeper of safety

You pore over paperwork, the daily documents
of ruined lives rebuilding themselves,
your eyes tired, the tea on your desk cooling

Every day you see it:
the bruised, betrayed face,
the intimacy of anger
distancing love

You try to stay objective,
but it's hard sometimes, like now,
when you're tired, your tea is cold,
and it's so very late in the engulfing darkness

41

MEASUREMENTS

The length of your body: 170 centimetres

The weight of your heart: 600 grams

The number of your regrets: 0

Of nails
you hammered into the deck: 1000

Of months
that you lived: 560, and 18 days

The depth of your unhappiness:
infinite

42

AN UNABRIDGED
HISTORY OF THE HEART

It beats

It stops beating

43

44

The Burrs of Paradise

45

46

1

Everywhere across the night sky
light punches through,
announces itself

Ah, the bold stars,
their bright audaciousness!

There was a time
he would have stood next to her,
admiring this

A time
when the fruits of paradise
were more plentiful than the burrs

2

Cardial meltdown:
the heart deliquescing
into a hot, bubbling anger,
its red aura of rage
visible (she thinks)
through the skin,
through the robe
she knots around her waist
like a tourniquet

She clicks on the lamp,
picks up the book
from the bedside table

The words sit in front of her
like so many black bugs,
page-pinned

Tonight she, too,
is going nowhere,
a dark butterfly
speared to her fate—
or her choice,
depending on your perspective

3

This is one of those relationships
in which only the man is allowed anger

The woman is allowed only patience
while he swings
his wide net of argument
over ten years,
triumphantly exhibits
his catch of examples,
all the things she's done wrong
slapped against her face
like wet fish

49

As she sits drinking
cup after cup of coffee
in the sullen night,
she's well aware of what she's done,
what she hasn't

Truth of self,
her only weapon

It demands to be permitted

It says: *Love despite all argument*

It says: *Leave although you love*

4

She tells him things about herself
but he doesn't believe them;
claims to know everything about her,
how she thinks, why she does what she does,
what she fears

And what he doesn't claim to know,
he suspects

His arrogance is astounding, sends
the part of her he originally loved
into hiding, like a fugitive

He sees only what he wants to see,
like the scientist
doctoring his own research,
finding, at any cost,
what he seeks

5

He prides himself on his peripheral vision,
his ability to register
what he thinks no one thinks he can see

She looks directly at him from behind,
watches him watching her
from the corner of his eye,
in this way the two of them
mirroring each other
endlessly

What he can't see:
the sun and moon in her
are heading for eclipse

51

6

He wears the chip on his shoulder
proudly, like an epaulette

He's angry,
and she'd better know it

She closes her eyes,
takes a vacation, vacates

Absence makes the heart grow calmer

Her absence, her heart,
the size of which should be irrelevant
but isn't

7

She's convinced
he should have been a lawyer

He interrupts, deliberately misinterprets,
shapes the testimony to fit the crime

The facts bray at his command;
arguing with him is useless

He's perfected
the cross-examination art,
the basic tenet: never ask why
unless you already know the answer

8

At dinner, lobster shell
slicing her thumb, butter
trickling hotly down her chin,
she asks him if he's dangerous

There are stories,
the man next door
who shoots his wife, kids, dog
unexpectedly, without reason

He was a quiet guy,
the neighbours say,
kept mostly to himself,
washed his car on Sundays

The lobster's claw is obvious

More frightening:
the boiled and bitter eye,
what's missing from it

9

"A Woman's Rhetorical Question Blues"

Baby, I can't take no more
can't take no more
can't take no more
so why do you insist?

Baby, I can't take no more
so why don't I resist?

55

10

A marriage is more than the sum of its starts

She wonders, as they make up yet again,
whether he's ever considered this

Marriage isn't a chicken-and-egg affair,
he used to say,
more like pigs and bacon

Think about it,
the difference in relationship:
chickens lay eggs,
pigs die giving bacon

Yes, she would answer,
it's the old question
of who wears the power in the family
and why

56

11

He lies down next to her
without touching

She swallows, pretends to wake;
constellates the night
into a brilliance in which the dark spaces
(from a distance) don't show

All is stars, full moon, shining

Her hands stutter along his body
like wounded birds

Something is elbowing in,
wants room to word itself

It isn't light

Finally, at the edge of sleep,
she looks down, sees
no abyss, nothing

It's like looking with open eyes
into a perfectly dark room

Whether the eyes are open or closed
makes no difference

12

Given darkness
the mind imagines light

Some call this madness;
others, hope

13

She has been sleepwalking for years
in the vicinity of this precipice,
has stumbled perilously close,
the danger unrecognized

Except in dreams
where his shadow stifles her
like a coffin lid, and her own
hovers uncertainly
in a background she can't see

Yet she can't resist,
can't help but wonder
what would happen if she took the chance,
leapt into the fear,
awakened

Would she see her shadow?

His?

14

She stands at the crossing,
a human semaphore,
her bell-strong voice, her flailing arms,
unheeded but necessary

She can't regulate
what comes from all directions, how fast,
but she signals warnings

No one knows that
she'd run against the train
if only she could move

15

The city is no longer the city

It is a natural landscape, an astonishing sea
where streetcars dive into subterranean caves,
their cries echoing like whale songs
in the quiet deep

She listens and is saved

Then dawn suddenly, winter

She's standing at an intersection,
waiting for a streetcar

61

No traffic

Fog, darkness,
snow falling

Finally it emerges, a bright eye
gradually magnified,
enormously neutral

She slips, falls, knows
she can't get up in time

If she'd spent her whole life
anticipating this moment,
would it have changed a thing?

16

She is obsessed with flight,
with birds, the stories of birds

How centuries ago it was believed
that birds of paradise flew
continuously around the sun,
touched earth
only when they died

Dreams them, thousand
upon radiant thousand,
a living ring of colour
breathing in the light

62

17

She comes upon him in the small light, moon
struggling through the window,
his self well hidden in sleep

She unfolds against his back with certainty

She is growing on despite him

63

The Persistence of Vision

To love the world with the eyes,
one uses them as hands.

Diane Ackerman, A Natural History of Love

HOW THE PHOTOGRAPH LIES:

Jack Ruby Shoots Lee Harvey Oswald, November 1963

> The image
> isn't responsible
> for our uses of it.

> *Adrienne Rich*

The shot
of Ruby shooting
Oswald, assassinating
the assassin, the two
inextricably linked
by this act, the proof
in the photograph
in which they are
forever framed

67

FIVE FACTS ABOUT PHOTOGRAPHY

No past or future,
just one
continuously present moment
framed by fate
and the photographer's eye,
serendipitous collusion

Beneath every photograph,
an invisible caption:
Who holds the camera?

The camera, like the gun,
has no motive: it's aimed,
it shoots

What matters:
light and motion,
how much, how little

Context is outside
the frame, always,
and there's no such thing
as a whole picture

PHOTOGRAPHING DARKNESS

Degrees of

Darkness that lengthens
the longer you look at it

Radical

Darkness that no light
can fully penetrate

Solid

Darkness that no eye
can dismantle

True

Darkness that hides
what it promises

HINDSIGHT

She heads out of one city toward another

It could be any city, the city
doesn't matter

The trunk of her small car
brims with cameras, tripods, flashes, film

She's listening to something rousing, symphonic
(*A Little Night Music* or Beethoven's *Ninth* perhaps)
her gaze on the road steady, her hands on the wheel
relaxed

Above her, airborne, you too are travelling
from one city to another

It could be any city, the city
doesn't matter

Your thoughts are starkly clear,
as they always are at high altitudes

In your lap: books, pens, sheets of paper
filled with words about men, a man,
relationship

The voice in your head says
Fix it or finish it

You listen

What neither you nor she
can possibly suspect:
that you will be in the same city,
and it will matter

71

SIGHT

What do you see? you ask
as you lay the photographs
one by one
on the kitchen table

I see canals, arches,
the exactness
of Venice on the day
your eyes were there

I see surprises of colour
in unexpected corners,
configurations of wall, complexity
of water

I see
your heart in the world,
light-written, profoundly
visible

VISUAL

The spring hues of the vineyard:
brown, yellow, beige,
hints of green;
the dark gnarly vines
twisting against the wires
like rebellious captives

The sun softens
the leftover winter barrenness

When together we look at the sky,
there is more of it,
and it is bluer

73

POETRY IS WHAT HAPPENS

> "Poetry is what happens when you look up
> from the page."
>
> *Gwendolyn MacEwen*

You
are what happened
when I looked up
from the page

74

GEOGRAPHY LESSON

Teach me the landscape that you love,
the west that is more than a direction

Teach me the shape of deer prints,
mystery of medicine wheels,
the stirrings of the vibrant earth
as it sings in stone and tree bark

Teach me the poetry between the rail lines

Teach me the true teal of the Bow River,
the nuances of light on wheat fields

Teach me the vertigo of pure prairie darkness,
its surprise of stars

A SPIRITUAL PASSION

Sometimes you enter the fire;
sometimes it enters you

Hypnotic arousal,
a slow taming, caress
of flank, fingers
through softest mane,
the deep gaze
not letting go, stroke
gently, hold
longer, sweet bondage

YOUR LOVE

Yesterday
your love was blue, the dark blue
of the peacock and the ocean

On other days
it is the two-toned green
of malachite, or the creamy white
of Devon custard

Sometimes
it is crimson or magenta,
the blood colours of birth

Some days
your love is bordered
by a premonition of roses
whose yellow petals glow like suns
before my eyes even open

Today
your love is black,
first colour of the soul,
and I cherish it

SANDPLAY

We're lazing, as we do each summer,
at Nickel Beach

I'm tracing memories in the sand
with a seagull feather

Here is Mexico, I say,
and here is the state of Jalisco,
and here Puerto Vallarta,
my mind moving from general to specific
like a zoom lens

Here is the Plaza las Glorias bar
and here (I pick up two stones,
move them about comically)
are you and I dancing

Later, as we lie
side by side, absorbing
the power of sand, a heat
that fits us perfectly, we imagine
Lake Erie is the Pacific
and a parasailor
will wing into view, Icarus
successful at last

We heal ourselves
through such dreams, take solace
from the sun, feel it
penetrate our foreheads

We listen
to the water sounds, stay
exquisitely still, the scent
of hibiscus lingering in our nostrils
as if we'd never left the tropical air

While behind closed eyes we wonder
which reality is more real

79

DRIVING AS AN ACT OF LOVE

You push down
on the gas, suddenly,
and hard

Reminds me
of take-off,
plane lifting, the elevator
drop
in the guts, excitement
of motion

You palm the gear shift,
your eyes
flick from the road
to me, *yes,* and
again
you accelerate, I feel
the pull of speed, come
close to arrival

MEMORY

You lean against the bar, order
two more beers, *Sol,*
taste of bright Mexico
on a cold Canadian night

Keep glancing back at her
through the layers of faces
crowding in behind you,
are drawn back always
to those eyes

When you return to her, she
kisses you deeply and you don't
care who might be watching
or where you are because
in that moment
she is all there is, and is

You want to bring her suns,
their incredible hopeful light,
forever

STUDIO SCENE

Picture this as a photo shoot

The backdrop is lowered,
winter seen
through large glass doors,
snow-mounds on the deck,
stark white on dark blue chairs

A woman in jeans and sweater
(also blue)
lies stretched on the green couch,
relaxed hunter

A cat sleeps at her feet

You are the photographer;
you notice things

The woman's hands,
their long, slender fingers;
her blue eyes
backlit by the January light;
the way her hair frames
her face; the shape
of her mouth, tilt of her chin,
the exact position of her body

The truth of her
in that moment

PHOTOGRAPH: THE WORLD

You send me a picture, taken
just hours before I dialled your number
on that pivotal November evening

From a space station, panoramic view,
the Earth at night, caught
with all its lights on

Our two cities
miniscule bright dots
within the glow fields, and us
within them, somewhere

Always of interest: what is made
invisible by distance, what is
revealed

It was as if, in those hours before
I phoned you, the universe
cleared, made space

And now, months later,
you send me
this picture of the world,
how it was, before
we re-connected

THE PERSISTENCE OF VISION
WITH REGARD TO MOVING OBJECTS

The human eye holds images
a fraction of a second longer
than they are in sight

Each such instant: an interstice
like the space between the shoe
and the foot in it, the act
and its consequence

After each frame, unnoticed,
the next moves in, smooth and discreet

The eye thinks it's looking
at one image only: illusion of motion

In this way my eyes hold you,
frame to frame to frame

Create their own illusion,
fill you in

NEGATIVE

The subject upside down,
light and dark reversed

The shadow truth
of what you see

85

I PREFERRED THE FANTASY

Your desk is by the window
on the fourth floor

I sit in the hotel bar
across the street, look up
at where I think you might be,
two panes of glass
and much space
between us

When I phone,
you move to the window, register
my blue sweater,
wave briefly

I finish my glass of red wine;
you do not reappear

You will look out again
only when I'm gone

LATE ONE NIGHT

Late one night at your apartment
you pull a photo from a previous life, the life
where I occupied a weekend only

There you are, you exactly,
the you I carried in my head for years,
but you're with someone else of course
(life moves on like water)

When I admire the picture
you tear it in two, rip yourself out
of context, hand me
the half with you in it, toss away
the other

Unfortunate, that
we can't crop ourselves from the past

Each time I look
at the edited photograph, I see
the other next to you, no longer there,
but there

CONSPICUOUS ABSENCES

At your apartment:

> not a photo of me
> in sight

> the stray hair on the pillow,
> removed

> the sheets and towels,
> laundered

> your red scarf sprayed with my perfume,
> lost

> the music we listened to,
> shelved

> the books I gave you,
> closed

> my e-mails and voice messages,
> deleted

There is not a sign of me
anywhere in your life

LIGHTING RATIO

You set me up, today's subject,
in the same room with yesterday's model

You've decided you want us both
in the picture

Light enters, either natural
or not

Consider the difference
between who receives the most light,
the least

Attend to intensity

This will affect contrast, softness,
the range of greys

It will also affect clarity

How much light
you allow, and what kind,
will determine the outcome
of the picture

I trust
that you know this

MONET AT GIVERNY

Water lilies, weeping willows, wisteria

Shadows vibrating
on the famous footbridge

His eyes obsessed for a lifetime
with the transformative power of light

His dream to master colour
as it masters him, to paint
exactly what he sees

90

But sight is fickle, alters
and distorts, weakens
and eventually fails

What's left: the vision
that never depended on the eyes

A PORTRAIT OF HOME

The choosing is what frames it: joy,
a sky address, habitat
of birds, clouds, all celestial bodies,
the harlequin beauty of light and darkness,
soul space, open

And in this, our days together
a graceful tessellation of sleep and waking,
peace, and
a startling tenderness

You are my place of wonder,
my continually arriving destination

Home, the choice I make
each moment

91

Acknowledgements

The phrase "the path of tender heroes" is used by the mystic poet Rumi.

"Photographing Darkness" arose out of a conversation with Anne Michaels.

The Burrs of Paradise appeared in its entirety in *The Harpweaver,* vol. 7, Summer 2000.
Some of the other poems were published in *Traffic East* (Buffalo, NY), *The Windsor Review, Writual,* and *Diviners.*

Thanks to Patricia Abram and Karen Lewis for their valuable comments on a number of the poems included here, and to artists Barbara Bickel and Linda Hankin for their enthusiasm for my "visual side."

Special thanks to a special group—in particular, Barb Fennessy, Darlene Hareguy, Ricki Heller, Jane Neily-Mallay and Kim Reid—whose unwavering support and kindness over many years have been, and continue to be, cherished gifts.

Finally, a huge thank-you to Elspeth Cameron for her unequivocal encouragement and her love.

SACRED DISASTERS

THE BURRS OF PARADISE

THE PERSISTENCE OF VISION

ACKNOWLEDGEMENTS